5 IN 1
POSITIVE AFFIRMATIONS & ACTIONS FOR
KINDESS, GRATITUDE, HEALTH, SELF LOVE and ENTREPRENEUR MINDSET

TurtlePublishing

Published by Turtle Publishing
All rights reserved.

Printed on demand in Australia, United States and United Kingdom.

Written & designed by Kathy Shanks
© Kathy Shanks 2021
Illustrations by Freepik Storyset & Turtle Publishing

No part of this publication may be reproduced, stored in a retrieval system, or transmitted in any form or by any means, electronic, mechanical, photocopying, recording or otherwise, without the prior written permission of the author.

Under no circumstances will any blame or legal responsibility be held against the publisher, or author, for any damages, reparation, or monetary loss due to the information contained within this book including, but not limited to — errors, omissions, or inaccuracies. Either directly or indirectly. You are responsible for your own choices, actions, and results.

Legal Notice: This book is copyright protected. This book is only for personal use. You cannot amend, distribute, sell, use, quote or paraphrase any part, or the content within this book, without the consent of the author or publisher.

Disclaimer: Please note the information contained within this document is for educational and entertainment purposes only. All effort has been executed to present accurate, up to date, and reliable, complete information. No warranties of any kind are declared or implied. Readers acknowledge that the author is not engaging in the rendering of legal, financial, medical or professional advice. The content within this book has been derived from various sources. Please consult a licensed professional before attempting any techniques outlined in this book.

SPECIAL BONUS
FREE BOOKS

FREE Workbook to begin an intentional journaling practice.

FREE 30 Days to Greater Self Love Program

Get FREE unlimited access to these AND all of my new books by joining our fan base!

SCAN WITH YOUR CAMERA OR GO TO
bit.ly/AffGifts

TABLE OF CONTENTS

How to use these books	*vii*
Gratitude	*3*
Self Love	*61*
Kindness	*119*
Health	*177*
Side Hustle	*235*

How to use these books

On the left-hand pages are affirmations. On the right-hand pages are actions for you to take.

You may like to work through this book one affirmation and action per day, or perhaps you'd like to trust divine guidance. Hold this book close to your heart or navel, close your eyes, take three gentle breaths, and as you breathe out on the third breath, open the book. We trust that you will be guided to the page you need the most.

POSITIVE AFFIRMATIONS AND ACTIONS FOR

Gratitude

PRACTICE POSITIVITY, HAPPINESS
AND MINDFULNESS WITH DAILY
RITUALS OF THANKFULNESS

Gratitude

Imagine your typical day.

You wake up bright and early and go about your morning rituals. Perhaps you kick off the day by whipping up some breakfast for yourself or your family before diving into everything else on your 'to-do' list. Most likely, the rest of the day is spent on things you *need* to do—maybe going to work, or taking care of the kids and making sure your household is in order, as well as running various seemingly never-ending errands. If you have a bit more time, maybe you're able to squeeze in the things you *want* to do—meeting up with friends, working on a hobby or personal project, or maybe getting in a quick workout.

No matter what your day looks like, chances are, you get by with a little help—from friends, family, and members of the community around you, the privileges and conveniences you enjoy, or even a greater force at work, be it nature, the universe, or any spiritual power.

Take that typical day, for example. The food on the table fuels you for the rest of your activities. The love from your significant other or your kids nourishes you, too, giving you a boost of motivation to carry with you. You might have teammates you collaborate with at work to produce amazing output. Even while out and about, say, at the supermarket or service centre, you encounter people who are ready to assist you in one way or another. Not to mention the *things* at your disposal—a car or public transport to get you where you need to go, your mobile to keep you connected, a place to call home.

There are *so many* people, things, and circumstances that support us and make each day possible. But, as we go about our daily lives, how often do we stop and express thanks? How much energy do we send towards gratitude?

It's all too easy to get caught up in both the hustle of our daily lives, as well as keeping sight of our long-term vision and goals. We rush from one thing to the next, barely having enough time for everything that has to get done, much less to take a step back and give thanks.

There's no denying that life can be *tough*, too. The difficulties, setbacks, and obstacles that are all an inevitable part of life can loom unfortunately large, blocking your view of the things that are going *right*—of everything else to be grateful for.

Despite these challenges, though, cultivating gratitude is incredibly important in living a full life. The truth is, it can be downright life-changing.

Nurturing a grateful heart allows contentment into your life. Instead of taking note of all that's lacking or that you still want, gratitude enables you to refocus on what you *already have*. It helps you get unstuck from 'what can be' and grounds you in 'what is.' You might be surprised at how happy you could be *right this moment*, just by recognising everything you have for what it truly is.

Not only does practising gratitude do wonders for you mentally and emotionally, but it actually impacts your physical health as well. Simply put, our thoughts, feelings, and actions engage different parts of the brain—pain activates a specific area, excitement taps another, and so on. Being grateful and recognising others' positive actions are processed in a region that's associated with socialisation and pleasure. Both of these are, in turn, connected to other parts of the brain that are responsible for stress relief and physical relaxation.

Gratitude is also extremely important in forming relationships and strengthening bonds with other people. Without even expressing thanks, *simply being* grateful involves recognising the positive impact others have on our lives and the ties that connect us with one another. Affirming *others* and the positive impact they have on your life galvanises your experience of being grateful. In expressing your sincere appreciation verbally or through any other means, you kindle the fire of gratitude within, keeping it burning brighter than ever. At its very core, gratitude pushes us to see the good in others.

In working towards more gratitude in your life, remember that it is a *practice*. Gratitude is more than a passive emotion—in fact, you probably subconsciously have that part of it covered already. After all, weren't we all brought up with good manners that include habitual, automatic 'thank you's?' Aren't we constantly taught to count our blessings?

True gratitude goes beyond that, though. It is a state of mindfulness combined with intentional action.

In exploring and cultivating a deeper sense of gratitude, an affirmation practice can allow you to pause and re-centre, focusing on the positivity in your life. It can be a powerful tool for identifying and really acknowledging each specific thing that you are grateful for.

> *"I am happy because I'm grateful. I choose to be grateful. That gratitude allows me to be happy."*
>
> - Will Arnett

GRATITUDE AFFIRMATIONS

With each day, the gratitude in my heart only grows.

I draw happiness from giving thanks.

I am overjoyed to be alive.

GRATITUDE ACTIONS

Before you go to bed, make a list of 5 good things that happened or that you experienced throughout the day.

Write a 'thank you' note to 3 people who have touched your life.

Begin each day with gratitude. Even before getting up and out of bed, give thanks for the new day.

GRATITUDE AFFIRMATIONS

I am grateful for my space in this world and the universe.

Recognising and giving thanks for everything I have is a part of who I am.

I am thankful for what I already have, and everything that I know is yet to come.

GRATITUDE ACTIONS

Practice being mindful and intentional each time you say 'thank you' to someone. Even for little everyday things, try to really let the gratitude wash over you as you say it.

Go on a walk outdoors and take notice of all the wonderful things you encounter along the way—the sights, sounds, sensations, and everything in between.

Write a 'thank you' letter to your past self—remember, you wouldn't be who you are today if not for them.

GRATITUDE AFFIRMATIONS

I am grateful for my body and everything it allows me to do.

I can always find something to be grateful for, no matter how small.

I honour and appreciate all the amazing people in my life.

GRATITUDE ACTIONS

Reflect on your journey so far. How has your life changed for the better in the past 5 years?

Spend quality time with your loved ones, just enjoying each other's company and being together.

Reach out to thank someone you have learned something from.

GRATITUDE AFFIRMATIONS

Gratitude holds tremendous power in my life.

My gratitude fuels and inspires me.

I am filled with gratitude for my journey so far, as well as the journey ahead.

GRATITUDE ACTIONS

Giving is gratitude in action. Do something nice for someone else as a way of 'paying it forward.'

Prepare a small token of appreciation for a service worker who regularly makes your life a little better.

Make a loved one their favourite meal.

GRATITUDE AFFIRMATIONS

I give thanks for the challenges that have shaped who I am.

My life is made infinitely richer by giving thanks for everything I have.

My grateful heart is beautiful.

GRATITUDE ACTIONS

Designate one day a week as your 'no complaints' day.

Set up a visual reminder of gratitude—a simple family memento or favourite snapshot will usually do the trick.

When faced with an obstacle or difficult situation, pause to ask yourself, "What can I learn from this?"

GRATITUDE AFFIRMATIONS

I am grateful for today.

Gratitude flows easily through all the areas of my life.

My mind is filled with appreciation for the world around me.

GRATITUDE ACTIONS

Share something you love—maybe a favourite song or book, or even just a recently discovered life hack—with a friend.

Set a timer for 60 seconds, and list down as many positive things in your life as you can in that minute.

Accept others' gratitude openly. Allow yourself to truly feel it when someone thanks you.

GRATITUDE AFFIRMATIONS

I am grateful for every breath that fills my lungs.

I love the life that I lead.

I am grateful to have the opportunity to impact others' lives positively.

GRATITUDE ACTIONS

Set aside some time each day to simply be present and reflect on the things you are grateful for.

Send someone a song that reminds you of them.

Think back to something that made you laugh out loud (or at least crack a really big smile) recently.

GRATITUDE AFFIRMATIONS

I live each day in awe of the universe.

Every day brings new chances to be grateful.

I begin and end each day with gratitude.

GRATITUDE ACTIONS

Write a letter to your personal hero. You can keep it to yourself or go ahead and send it to them—it's totally up to you.

Listen to a song that brings you back to one of your favourite moments ever.

Write down the 3 biggest lessons you are grateful to have learned so far in life.

GRATITUDE AFFIRMATIONS

I approach life with a sense of wonder.

I never take anything for granted.

I find huge joy in even the smallest of things.

GRATITUDE ACTIONS

Have you recently purchased from a small business or tried a local restaurant? Write a glowing review of something you enjoyed.

What are you excited about? Write down what you are looking forward to in the next week, month, and year.

Write about your favourite memory with your best friend and share it with them.

GRATITUDE AFFIRMATIONS

I am perfectly content with where I am in life.

I recognise all the privileges that I am blessed with.

I am grateful to be able to pursue my passions in life.

GRATITUDE ACTIONS

Tell your friends and family you love them whenever you feel it—say it out loud and without hesitation.

Set aside a few minutes to practice or exercise a skill you're grateful to have.

Write a letter of gratitude for your hopes for your future. Use gratitude to manifest your dreams.

GRATITUDE AFFIRMATIONS

I am beyond thankful for my family, friends, and loved ones.

With every breath, I give thanks.

I focus on the good and let go of the bad.

GRATITUDE ACTIONS

After attending events like birthday celebrations or dinner parties, make it a habit to send handwritten notes of appreciation to the hosts.

Make time to cuddle with your partner, kids, pets… anyone you're grateful to love and be loved by.

Organise your favourite photos into albums or maybe even a creative collage you can frame and hang up on the wall.

GRATITUDE AFFIRMATIONS

I turn my gratitude into action.

My life is filled with things to be grateful for.

I find peace in gratitude.

GRATITUDE ACTIONS

Show appreciation for a friend or relative by putting together a personalised care package for them.

Write about the last time you felt completely content and happy.

Go somewhere you can really immerse in nature—the beach or mountains are always a great idea. While you're there, take a moment to reflect on how it feels to be part of this great big world.

GRATITUDE AFFIRMATIONS

I am grateful for the room I still have for growth.

My existence is meaningful and purposeful.

I trust what life has in store for me.

GRATITUDE ACTIONS

Take someone on a tour of all your favourite spots in your neighbourhood.

Do you have a mentor, coach, or teacher who has made a profound impact on your life? Reach out to them and let them know how much you appreciate them.

Even just for a day, take over the chores usually done by someone else in your household.

GRATITUDE AFFIRMATIONS

I am grateful for my talents, skills, and abilities.

The universe favours me and supports me.

I am grateful for every person who has touched my life in some way, whether big or small.

GRATITUDE ACTIONS

Tip generously whenever you enjoy exceptional service at a restaurant.

At work, publicly thank and maybe even officially acknowledge someone who helped you out with something or contributed to your team's efforts.

Come up with a list of 5 positive things in your life that you might be taking for granted—dig deep. How do these make your life better? How can you be more mindfully appreciative of these moving forward?

GRATITUDE AFFIRMATIONS

Gratitude comes naturally to me.

I am proud of my grateful heart and mind.

Gratitude uplifts me and sets me up for success.

GRATITUDE ACTIONS

Think of your least favourite part of the day or week. Now, try to find something positive about it.

Show your body appreciation for everything it does for you by fuelling up with a meal that's both delicious and healthy.

Write about something you have worked hard for and that you are grateful to have finally gotten or achieved.

GRATITUDE AFFIRMATIONS

I allow gratitude to transform my soul for the better.

Gratitude opens doors for great things to come into my life.

I am grateful for all the things I am given a chance to experience in this life—good, bad, and everything in between.

GRATITUDE ACTIONS

Get a deeper appreciation for the food you enjoy by taking a 'field trip' to your local farm.

What's a memorable tradition you appreciated growing up? How can you bring this back now in your adult life?

Think of someone you love, and list down 10 of your favourite things about them.

GRATITUDE AFFIRMATIONS

I accept challenges with a grateful heart, as these are opportunities to grow.

The positive energy of gratitude radiates deep within my soul.

I invite the seeds of gratitude to take root in my soul.

GRATITUDE ACTIONS

Put on your favourite song, and jot down a description of how it makes you feel.

Write about the biggest obstacle you've overcome in your life.

Experience something—go somewhere you've never been before, try a new activity—for the first time.

GRATITUDE AFFIRMATIONS

I am thankful for the material possessions I have.

I am grateful for a place to rest and refill my cup.

I am grateful that my needs are met each day.

GRATITUDE ACTIONS

Reflect on why gratitude is important to you. You could meditate on it, write down your thoughts, or talk it out with someone else—whatever works best for you.

Have lunch out with your colleagues or teammates.

Find a piece of art—music, movie, book, painting, any other medium—that resonates with you and learn about the inspiration or story behind it.

GRATITUDE AFFIRMATIONS

I am aligned with the forces of gratitude in the world.

I raise my vibrations with gratitude.

I express gratitude loudly and with pride.

GRATITUDE ACTIONS

Visit a nearby park or any outdoor spot where you can sit and watch the world carry on around you. Stay for a bit and make a mental note of all the positive things you observe.

Think about your favourite scent. Write about how it makes you feel or what memories it calls to mind.

What's the best piece of advice you've ever received? Pass it along to someone else.

GRATITUDE AFFIRMATIONS

Life is good.

I hold on to gratitude through both highs and lows.

I choose to see the best in others.

GRATITUDE ACTIONS

Keep a gratitude journal and take time to list the positive things you experience every day.

Tidy up your favourite spot or treasured personal space at home.

List down 5 things you're grateful for in the city you live in.

GRATITUDE AFFIRMATIONS

I appreciate every new day as a beautiful gift.

I choose gratitude mindfully and with the utmost intention.

I am in awe of all the forces of nature.

GRATITUDE ACTIONS

At places you regularly frequent, learn the servers' or staff's first names and make it a point to use these.

Take a moment to recognise how you are a blessing in others' lives.

Right this very moment, stop and look around you. What's one beautiful, inspiring, or overall positive thing you notice?

GRATITUDE AFFIRMATIONS

I am grateful for all the love in my life and every expression of love that comes my way.

Gratitude brings me a deep sense of joy and happiness.

I am eternally grateful for my very existence.

GRATITUDE ACTIONS

In the coming week, share 3 of your simplest pleasures with others.

Close your eyes, place your palm on your chest and feel your heartbeat. Take a quiet moment to appreciate what it means to be alive.

Write about something that gives you hope and makes you optimistic about the future.

GRATITUDE AFFIRMATIONS

My soul sings with gratitude.

The more thankful I am, the more content I become.

I am grateful to have a job that sustains me.

GRATITUDE ACTIONS

Dedicate a social media post to celebrating your spouse or best friend.

Give your boss or client a random token of appreciation.

Think of a time someone had your back. How might you do the same for someone else?

GRATITUDE AFFIRMATIONS

I appreciate all the sources of positivity in my life.

I am always sincere in my expressions of thanks.

I appreciate everything I have exactly for what it is—nothing more, and nothing less.

GRATITUDE ACTIONS

Thinking of the kids in your life, what can you learn from them and how they see the world?

List down 5 things that bring you comfort.

Make it a point to eat meals mindfully, really savouring and appreciating the tastes and sensations of your food.

GRATITUDE AFFIRMATIONS

I am grateful for the abundance of good that permeates every aspect of my life.

There is something to be grateful for everywhere I go, and in everything I see.

I choose to flourish and grow in gratitude.

GRATITUDE ACTIONS

When faced with 'challenging' individuals and people you don't quite get along the best with, try to list down 3 positive things about them in your head.

Write about your best childhood memory.

Ask a close friend or loved one to share one of their favourite memories with you.

POSITIVE AFFIRMATIONS AND ACTIONS FOR
Self Love

LEARN TO LOVE YOURSELF, CREATE HAPPINESS, IMPROVE YOUR CONFIDENCE & BUILD INNER STRENGTH

Self Love

One of the first things we learn as a child is to love others. Growing up, we're constantly reminded to be kind and helpful to the people around us. It's no surprise that somewhere along the way, many of us learn that selflessness is a prized virtue and that putting ourselves and our own needs before others is selfish—something to be avoided at all costs.

Now, there's absolutely nothing wrong with treating others with love and kindness—there can never be enough of it in the world! But, to be a light in someone else's life, you've got to *kindle your own spark first*. Everything starts with loving yourself.

Self-love is such a powerful force. Not only does your capacity to care for others grow as you care for yourself, but so does your overall wellbeing. Whether you notice it or not, constantly putting yourself last on your list of priorities and pushing your own needs to the bottom of the pile takes a considerable toll on your happiness. If you're feeling tired, drained, or overwhelmed, perhaps it's time to give yourself the love and care *you* undoubtedly deserve.

Self-love is much more than a feeling or a mere state of being. It's a *commitment* to tend to your own needs and do things to fill your cup. It means actively being compassionate towards yourself, accepting who you are, and celebrating your authentic self… flaws and all.

In a world where we're wired to chase relentlessly after success—*whatever* our vision of that is—cultivating self-love can definitely be tough. We tend to be hardest on ourselves, struggling under the pressure to become our best selves and measuring our own worth against where we are in relation to our goals.

Here's the thing, though: self-love is unconditional.

We are already worthy, wherever we are in our respective journeys. We are all *enough*. Self-love shouldn't have to wait until you land your dream job, achieve the 'perfect' body, or make the 'right' connections. True self-love meets you where you're at, *just as you are*.

It's important to recognise that loving yourself doesn't just happen overnight. It's a journey in itself—a dynamic process of unlearning negative, limiting beliefs and behaviour and replacing these with a healthy self-care practice.

This could mean different things to different people. Everyone expresses and receives love differently, and self-love is no exception.

No matter what your own personal path looks like, though, affirmations can be extremely valuable along the way.

Thought patterns are rooted in actual connections in the brain—repeatedly thinking something strengthens its specific pathway and triggers a chemical response that makes it easier to default to later on. This simply means that words hold power, and affirmations can be a great way to harness this.

The very act of repeating affirmations to yourself allows you to explore a reflective, meditative state. This alone can calm the mind, helping relieve any anxiety and the stress of day to day life.

As consistent self-affirmation practice reinforces your sense of self and allows you to identify what you truly value in life, it can also be an amazing way to boost your confidence and build a foundation of self-belief.

Finally, and perhaps most importantly, affirmations can also help you find joy in both the person you are, and who you are still striving to be. Positive self-talk *unlocks* a deep sense of contentment and happiness from within. At the same time, it keeps you motivated and empowers you to focus your energy and send it towards your goals.

By setting aside time each day for some positive self-talk or simply keeping a couple of affirmations in your back pocket to call to mind whenever you need them, you can take control of your wellbeing and drive your own narrative.

It doesn't have to be fancy—you can choose to say the statements out loud, write the ones that resonate with you the most in your journal, or just close your eyes and focus on the words quietly.

Combined with conscious, mindful (and fun!) self-care activities and exercises, repeating these powerful statements to yourself regularly creates new, healthy patterns—ones that allow you to nourish your mind, body, heart, and soul.

"Demonstrate love by giving it, unconditionally, to yourself. And as you do, you will attract others into your life who will love you without conditions."

- **Paul Ferrini**

SELF-LOVE AFFIRMATIONS

I love who I am, and I'm excited about who I am becoming.

My thoughts and feelings matter.

I am worthy of love and affection.

SELF-LOVE ACTIONS

Pick some affirmations that really resonate with you, and practice saying these out loud to yourself in front of the mirror each day.

Once a week, treat yourself to something you really, truly enjoy.

Run a luxurious bath with your favourite scent and give yourself as much time as you want to enjoy it.

SELF-LOVE AFFIRMATIONS

I accept myself wholly, flaws and all.

I am happy to be uniquely me.

I deserve to spend time and energy on things that make me happy.

SELF-LOVE ACTIONS

List down 10 things you are proud of about your character and who you are.

List down 10 things you adore about your body.

Create a bedtime ritual that helps you wind down and relax. It doesn't have to take long or be complicated—it can be as simple as having a cup of tea or listening to a soothing song.

SELF-LOVE AFFIRMATIONS

My needs are important and deserve attention.

I am deeply committed to caring for myself.

I am capable of setting healthy boundaries for myself.

SELF-LOVE ACTIONS

Put on some of your favourite upbeat music, turn it up, and dance!

It's time to finally get rid of those clothes in the depths of your closet that no longer fit.

Time for a social media audit—unfollow any accounts or influencers that make you feel bad about yourself or don't add any value to your life.

SELF-LOVE AFFIRMATIONS

I am allowed to put myself first.

I am wonderful and special.

I deserve rest whenever I need it.

SELF-LOVE ACTIONS

Make moisturising a post-shower habit—give yourself a little massage while you're at it!

Re-read your favourite childhood book.

Spend a rainy or chilly day curled up with a mug of your favourite hot beverage and a good book.

SELF-LOVE AFFIRMATIONS

I deserve the space that I occupy in this world.

I accept and love my imperfections because they are part of what makes me who I am.

I have the power to lift myself up.

SELF-LOVE ACTIONS

Create a personal nook for yourself at home. It can be as simple as setting a comfortable chair by a window and adding your favourite blanket or pillow.

Write down the best compliment you've ever received.

Try a new hairstyle or fashion trend you've had your eye on for a while.

SELF-LOVE AFFIRMATIONS

I honour my inner power.

Every part of me is worthy of respect.

I am allowed to be proud of my accomplishments and celebrate these.

SELF-LOVE ACTIONS

Go out for a meal by yourself and focus on enjoying your own company.

Start a daily mood tracker on your phone or in your journal.

Try to revive an old hobby or interest that you were forced to drop for whatever reason.

SELF-LOVE AFFIRMATIONS

I create my own journey and my own story.

I am filled with light and grace.

I am both infinitely loved and loving.

SELF-LOVE ACTIONS

Put on your favourite party outfit (you know, the one you don't get enough opportunities to wear) to lounge around at home.

Do an at-home spa day with a DIY face or hair mask.

Find and learn a breathing exercise that works for you, and use it whenever you need a little pocket of calm in your day.

SELF-LOVE AFFIRMATIONS

I let go of thoughts that do not serve me.

I allow all negativity, pain, or anxiety to fall away from me.

With every breath, I welcome in love, light, and happiness.

SELF-LOVE ACTIONS

Can you go an entire day without checking social media? Try it out and see how it makes you feel.

Allow yourself to fall down a rabbit hole of funny or cute videos online for a bit.

Start that book that you've been meaning to get around to.

SELF-LOVE AFFIRMATIONS

I release any expectations I feel pressured to live up to.

I am a child of the universe.

I am worthy of love and affection.

SELF-LOVE ACTIONS

List down 5 things you're capable of that not many people can do.

How long has it been since you've walked barefoot outdoors, on the grass or at the beach?

Designate one day a month where you have absolutely nothing planned. Feel free to spend that day lazing about or just going with the flow.

SELF-LOVE AFFIRMATIONS

I am fully capable of standing on my own two feet.

I am a beautiful person inside and out.

I deserve all the happiness in the world.

SELF-LOVE ACTIONS

If you have a junk drawer or a specific long-standing pile of clutter in your house, now's the time to get around to organising it finally.

Re-read your old journals or posts just to appreciate how far you've come.

Make time to hang out with a friend who's fun to be around.

SELF-LOVE AFFIRMATIONS

I love my body, including its flaws and imperfections.

I am enough, always and in all ways.

I am filled with grit and determination.

SELF-LOVE ACTIONS

Take a makeup-free, filterless selfie and find 5 things you love about it.

Plan a day trip or vacation—it doesn't matter if it's happening soon or if you even end up going or not. Just have fun with dreaming it all up!

What makes you feel like your best self? List down everything you can think of.

SELF-LOVE AFFIRMATIONS

I rise to every challenge in my own unique way.

I am more than my past mistakes.

I am proud to be my own cheerleader.

SELF-LOVE ACTIONS

On your next grocery trip, pick up one fun food item you wouldn't normally buy.

Sleep in on a weekend morning!

Listen to your favourite album from start to finish.

SELF-LOVE AFFIRMATIONS

I am in control of my own happiness.

Fear cannot stand in my way.

I am alive and flourishing.

SELF-LOVE ACTIONS

As part of your nighttime routine, take time to gently and thoroughly cleanse your face and 'take the day off.'

List down 5 healthy boundaries or non-negotiables that you would like to start enforcing.

You don't need a reason to buy yourself flowers!

SELF-LOVE AFFIRMATIONS

I am a one-of-a-kind work of art.

I sow seeds of love in the darkest parts of myself.

The light of my soul amazes me.

SELF-LOVE ACTIONS

Turn your afternoon coffee into a treat with a cinnamon stick, a sprinkle of cocoa powder, or a dollop of whipped cream.

Give your room or any personal space a makeover. Rearrange your furniture, paint an accent wall, or just hang up some colourful new curtains—it's all up to you, and it doesn't have to be anything major.

Listen to an uplifting, motivating song. Close your eyes, and enjoy how the music makes you feel.

SELF-LOVE AFFIRMATIONS

I exude beauty and grace.

Confidence comes naturally to me.

There is nobody else in this world exactly like me.

SELF-LOVE ACTIONS

The next time you eat out, give yourself permission to order that dessert.

Belt out your favourite tunes!

Re-watch a favourite movie or episode of a series.

SELF-LOVE AFFIRMATIONS

My heart is strong and proud.

I tap into a deep awareness of who I am.

I listen closely to the song of my soul.

SELF-LOVE ACTIONS

Describe your superpower.

Ask for a big hug from someone who gives you comfort.

When you're feeling stressed or anxious, let it all go on paper—list down everything that's weighing on your mind.

SELF-LOVE AFFIRMATIONS

Loving energy surrounds me.

I am safe in the universe's embrace.

I am perfectly imperfect.

SELF-LOVE ACTIONS

Write about feeling beautiful in your own skin, whether it's a moment you've experienced or just how that might feel regularly.

Set aside a few minutes each day to simply get lost in your own thoughts—you can even set an actual timer or alarm if that works for you.

Practice always receiving compliments openly and graciously. Even when you feel you don't deserve them, accept them with a bright smile and a sincere 'thank you!'

SELF-LOVE AFFIRMATIONS

I am rooted in goodness and rising towards the light.

The loudest voice in my life is my own.

I am at peace with the past, present, and future.

SELF-LOVE ACTIONS

If possible, open all your windows and curtains to let fresh air in.

What do you feel you need more of in your life? What's stopping you from getting or having that?

Re-evaluate your relationships. Ask yourself if it might be time to let go of or stop investing emotionally in those that bring toxicity and negativity into your life.

SELF-LOVE AFFIRMATIONS

I am capable of so much more than I ever dreamed.

My soul always finds its way.

Negative energy has no place in my life.

SELF-LOVE ACTIONS

Make a 'happy jar' by writing down little treats for yourself on slips of paper, mixing up tangible things like "have a chocolate bar" with activities like "phone your favourite person." Every time you need a dose of positivity, pick something out of the jar.

Give yourself permission to say 'no' to something.

Get down on the floor to just play and roll around with your pet.

SELF-LOVE AFFIRMATIONS

Joy begins within me.

I am allowed to move and grow at my own pace.

I express myself confidently with pride and joy.

SELF-LOVE ACTIONS

List down 3 things you'd like to forgive yourself for... and try to work on following through.

The next time a negative thought about yourself pops into your head, imagine saying it to or about someone you love. Chances are, you'll be able to turn that thought right around.

Paint your fingernails and toenails a bright, happy colour you've always wanted to try.

SELF-LOVE AFFIRMATIONS

I respect myself deeply and completely.

I love myself unconditionally.

I am worthy of the utmost care and compassion.

SELF-LOVE ACTIONS

Treat yourself to new bedsheets.

When you least feel like it, take a deep breath and put on the biggest smile you can muster—it won't be long until you begin to feel your mood lift as well.

Wash and deep condition your hair.

SELF-LOVE AFFIRMATIONS

My capacity to love grows each day.

I honour my unique journey.

Loving myself is a process.

SELF-LOVE ACTIONS

Every day, make it a point to do one good thing for your mind, body, and heart.

Make a creative collage, illustration, or even just a written list of all your favourite things. What's your favourite movie? Colour? Season? Place? Food? What else can you think of that makes you the absolute happiest?

Look up an interesting cocktail (or mocktail) and make yourself one to enjoy after a long workday.

SELF-LOVE AFFIRMATIONS

I protect the unique spark within.

I am always changing for the better.

I release anger to make room for love.

SELF-LOVE ACTIONS

Write down 3 things you don't like about yourself. Then, rewrite them into positive, affirming statements.

Grab yourself a healthy, energising mid-afternoon snack.

Remember that needing support isn't a weakness—reach out for help whenever you need it.

SELF-LOVE AFFIRMATIONS

I am fuelled by love and filled with joy.

This wonderful path of mine is unlike any other.

I am braver than I could have ever imagined.

SELF-LOVE ACTIONS

Doodle without worrying about it looking good or turning out well.

Learn about your love language.

Go on a relaxing drive through your favourite neighbourhood.

SELF-LOVE AFFIRMATIONS

I stand by my truth, always.

I trust my wisdom and honour my intuition.

I free myself from every doubt and fear.

SELF-LOVE ACTIONS

Make yourself a full-course meal at home.

Try not to scroll through your phone in bed, whether first thing in the morning or while waiting to fall asleep.

After a long day, take your time and be mindful about how it feels to change out of your work outfit and into your favourite comfortable clothes.

Kindness
is my Superpower

POSITIVE AFFIRMATIONS & ACTIONS FOR
IMPROVING YOUR SELF-WORTH, HAPPINESS,
EMPATHY, GRATITUDE & SELF-LOVE

Kindness

Imagine if every single person treated each other with empathy, generosity, and compassion. Imagine if judgment, prejudice, or discrimination simply didn't exist. Imagine a world where kindness is so commonplace that it's the norm. Wouldn't that be exactly the kind of world you'd want to live in?

But, let's face it: the fact is, it isn't always easy to be kind.

Most of the time, we simply forget to be kind—it's not like we go out of our way to be awful to other people. Chances are, we're not even unkind, exactly, just… disengaged. We're just so preoccupied with working hard to make sure our own (or our families') needs are met that we can't even begin to think of extending ourselves to others.

Often, being in a constant rush to take care of the many things on our plates can also be overwhelming and stressful. Sometimes, this can lead to less-than-ideal choices regarding how we deal with those around us. You know those instances—those moments when you pick a fight with your partner or snap at your toddler over the littlest of things at the end of a long, exhausting day.

Perhaps worse than being too busy for kindness is how we've become jaded and cynical. With time, the realities of the world have made us hard—we know all about the negativity and darkness that's undeniably out there. We see it on the news, or sometimes firsthand, around us, and sadly, it all has taught us to do everything we can to protect ourselves. Being kind comes with a certain vulnerability that can be hard to open ourselves up to.

There's also no denying that it can be difficult sometimes to see our differences through the lens of understanding. Whatever these differences may be—whether in how we think or act, what we look like or believe—kindness can often require us to put ourselves in each other's shoes. That is definitely no easy feat.

So, we all want a kinder world, but it can sometimes feel impossible to achieve. Not only is putting it in motion a challenge, but you might even find yourself thinking, "I'm just one person, after all. What difference could I possibly make?"

Well, to put it in perspective: have you ever been on the receiving end of someone else's kindness, especially on a particularly bad day? Maybe a co-worker randomly complimented your hair at a time when you didn't feel the least bit attractive. Or, perhaps a stranger held the elevator door for you and saved you from being late to a meeting. It cost them no more than 15 seconds, and they probably did it without thinking… and yet it made all the difference to you, right? You can never know what others are going through—don't underestimate the impact you're capable of making in other people's lives. And, perhaps more importantly, the ripples you can put in motion.

The thing about kindness is that it doesn't have to be big. Being kind doesn't have to mean donating all your money to charity or dedicating your life to volunteering. The truth is, it very rarely takes the form of a grand gesture.

In fact, one of the most effective forms of kindness is being kind to yourself. To even begin to share yourself— your time, resources, talents—with others, you first have to fill your own cup. This only comes with consistently treating yourself with respect and love.

Whether towards yourself or others, practising kindness is all about starting small and doing things with intention. While it can sometimes be easy to confuse being nice with being kind, the two aren't the same—you can lend a helping hand while being resentful about it. Kindness goes beyond behaviour. It entails cultivating a spirit of generosity, empathy, and compassion.

Because kindness starts from within before radiating outwards, affirmations can be powerful tools to kindle this spirit.

Our brains are wired to 'take note of' patterns of thinking we consistently use and 'remember' these for easy access later on. The more we repeat certain things in our minds, the more natural it becomes for us to harness these later on.

Whether you choose to say them out loud, write them down in a journal, or just focus on them mentally, regularly repeating these short statements can help you focus your energy on positivity. A regular affirmation practice can help you re-centre on the essential values you hold in your heart and know to be true.

Of course, kindness must eventually find its way out into the world in the form of action. Again, remember that even the smallest, simplest things can make a huge difference, as long as they are done mindfully and with heart.

Kindness can change the world… and it all starts within each of us.

"Be kind to others, so that you may learn the secret art of being kind to yourself."

- Paramahansa Yogananda

KINDNESS AFFIRMATIONS

I am generous with my gifts and use these to lift others up.

I treat others with compassion.

I am always willing to lend a helping hand to those who need it.

KINDNESS ACTIONS

Make it a point to consciously do at least one selfless thing each and every day. It doesn't matter if it's big or small, as long as it is done with heartfelt intention.

Compliment people freely, genuinely, and often.

Host a nice dinner or get together for some of your closest friends.

KINDNESS AFFIRMATIONS

I am a loving, giving person.

Being able to positively impact someone else makes me happy.

I love seeing others succeed.

KINDNESS ACTIONS

Send a sincere message of support to someone you think might be in need of it.

Write about an instance someone was kind to you—the positive impact they had on your life or even just on your day, how it made you feel, and what you learned from it.

Brighten up a co-worker's morning by surprising them with coffee.

KINDNESS AFFIRMATIONS

I am happy to celebrate my loved ones' triumphs right along with them.

I am sensitive to the needs of others.

I am excited to inspire and empower those around me.

KINDNESS ACTIONS

If you're qualified and able, donate blood.

Leave little sticky notes with messages of encouragement or uplifting quotes where strangers might unexpectedly find them.

Support small local businesses—trying out their offerings and spreading the word go a long way.

KINDNESS AFFIRMATIONS

I am a safe space for those who need it.

Giving brings me joy.

I am a source of joy and positivity for others.

KINDNESS ACTIONS

Volunteer at your local animal shelter.

Clean out your closet and donate items that are still in good shape to a homeless shelter or local charity.

Along with (or even instead of) traditional presents, make meaningful donations to chosen charities in your loved ones' names for their birthdays.

KINDNESS AFFIRMATIONS

I am mindful of speaking from a place of positivity.

My heart is gracious and forgiving.

I treat everyone equally, regardless of our wonderful differences.

KINDNESS ACTIONS

Write about an act of kindness you witnessed recently.

Hand out cold beverages to your mailmen, garbage collectors, or delivery persons on hot days.

Visit an aged care home and just spend time hanging out and chatting with an elderly person in need of a friend.

KINDNESS AFFIRMATIONS

I am kind not only in my actions but also in my thoughts and words.

I am a thoughtful friend.

I find joy in bringing out the best in other people.

KINDNESS ACTIONS

'Adopt' or sponsor wildlife online or make a donation to an ecological conservation project.

Phone a friend you haven't talked to in a while just to check in on them and catch up.

Hug a family member or friend when they need it the most.

KINDNESS AFFIRMATIONS

I am happy when I can make someone else smile.

I treat every single person around me with respect.

I always listen genuinely and try to keep an open mind, even with beliefs or opinions that are different from mine.

KINDNESS ACTIONS

Be someone's sounding board or even shoulder to cry on.

Read a child their favourite book.

Practice noticing those around you who are struggling or having a rough time. You might not always be in a position to help them, but extending a little empathy and extra patience goes a long way.

KINDNESS AFFIRMATIONS

When I give, I do it freely and wholeheartedly.

I put my heart into helping others.

I am a good listener.

KINDNESS ACTIONS

Bring over a meal to share with a friend or family member who lives alone.

Hold the door or elevator for someone.

Carve out at least 10 minutes each day just to show yourself some love in whatever way you choose.

KINDNESS AFFIRMATIONS

I am 100% present when I am with people I care about.

I am love embodied.

I fill my cup so I can keep being a blessing to others.

KINDNESS ACTIONS

Offer to babysit for a friend or relative.

Spread positivity online—repost, reblog, or share things that made you smile!

Buy someone flowers… just because.

KINDNESS AFFIRMATIONS

I fuel my actions with love.

I truly enjoy setting others up for success.

I am a light in someone's darkness

KINDNESS ACTIONS

Is there someone in your life you owe an apology to? Write a heartfelt letter to give them whenever you're ready.

Share your skills or knowledge with someone without asking for anything in return. It could be anything from simply answering a co-worker's question to the best of your abilities, to helping a neighbour out with a home improvement project.

Let someone else take over the playlist during a long drive.

KINDNESS AFFIRMATIONS

I speak up and stand against injustice.

I move from a place of empathy and understanding.

I genuinely enjoy lending a helping hand.

KINDNESS ACTIONS

Surprise your partner with an amazing breakfast in bed.

Every time you buy a new non-necessity for yourself, donate an old belonging—anything, really—to someone in need.

Greet waiters, retail staff, and other customer service workers with a sincere smile.

KINDNESS AFFIRMATIONS

I am supportive, uplifting, and motivating.

I refuse to speak ill of others behind their backs.

I am patient and considerate.

KINDNESS ACTIONS

If you know someone who's moving house or doing some major home renovations, offer to help out.

Participate in a community cleanup activity or neighbourhood recycling drive.

Challenge yourself to compliment a stranger!

KINDNESS AFFIRMATIONS

I am filled with boundless love for those around me.

I refuse to let fear get in the way of love and kindness.

I live life with an open, ever-expanding heart.

KINDNESS ACTIONS

Happy with the service you received at a shop or restaurant? Take note of your server or attendant's name and put in a good word for them with their manager.

When a conversation you're in starts to veer towards gossip or negativity, try your best to turn it around or change the topic.

Always remember your pleases and thank yous.

KINDNESS AFFIRMATIONS

I am proud of the positivity I put out into the world.

I radiate love and goodness.

By allowing myself to be led by love, I cannot fail.

KINDNESS ACTIONS

Sign up to be an official organ donor.

Learn about another culture—if you have a friend or colleague who belongs to that culture who's willing to share, even better!

Comment on friends' social media posts with sincere compliments and uplifting words.

KINDNESS AFFIRMATIONS

I am always ready to stand strong for those who cannot.

I have so much to give and share.

Every life is equally, tremendously precious.

KINDNESS ACTIONS

Send a couple of friends some handwritten snail mail. Better yet, surprise them with some lovely postcards even if you're from the same city!

Don't be afraid to get vocal about causes you are passionate about.

Do your best to talk about ideas, not people.

KINDNESS AFFIRMATIONS

I am kind without condition.

I am so blessed to be able to share with others.

My capacity for loving others is limitless.

KINDNESS ACTIONS

Remember that confrontation doesn't necessarily have to be a negative thing. In situations where you need to call someone out, check yourself and make sure you are coming from a place of love and a genuine desire to uplift others.

Leave little notes of love and affection around the house for your partner to find unexpectedly.

If someone asks you a question you don't readily know the answer to, take the time to look it up and get back to them.

KINDNESS AFFIRMATIONS

I am happy to set the stage for others to shine.

I let go of all my negative biases and preconceived notions of others.

I value and cherish the trust others put in me.

KINDNESS ACTIONS

Make something for someone. It can be anything (a poem or song, handmade jewellery, a batch of cookies… anything), as long as you made it yourself and put your heart into it.

Ask a loved one about their goals. How can you support their journey in your own little way? What can you do to help them achieve those goals?

If you have kids (or any children in your life), encourage them to donate their old toys and books.

KINDNESS AFFIRMATIONS

Each person on this earth is uniquely beautiful and unique.

I cultivate peace in any way I can.

Kindness is what makes the world a beautiful place.

KINDNESS ACTIONS

Sign petitions for causes you care about.

Hand over the remote control to someone else and let them have free reign over family TV time.

Sign up for a charity run.

KINDNESS AFFIRMATIONS

I accept others just as they are.

I am my best self when I help others.

I always try to see where someone is coming from.

KINDNESS ACTIONS

Put 'stray' groceries back where they belong as often as you can when you spot them at the store.

Pack an extra snack or lunch to take to the office and share with a co-worker.

Tape a bit of change to a random vending machine.

KINDNESS AFFIRMATIONS

I approach conflict with compassion.

I have the power to change someone's life for the better.

My gentleness is my strength.

KINDNESS ACTIONS

Stop for a talented busker or street performer. Don't forget to give them a generous donation afterwards.

Share your favourite recipe with someone who loves to cook.

Try out eco-friendly, sustainable swaps for some everyday items such as straws and single-use plastic containers.

KINDNESS AFFIRMATIONS

I accept that sometimes, kindness means saying 'no'.

I let go of any grudges or past conflicts.

Each day holds endless opportunities to be kind.

KINDNESS ACTIONS

Leave some change at the laundromat for strangers.

Go out of your way to make a new friend.

Pick up extra chores around the house without being asked.

KINDNESS AFFIRMATIONS

I am grateful for the things I can share.

Kindness comes to me effortlessly and without burden.

I advocate for the weak and less fortunate.

KINDNESS ACTIONS

Set up a bird or butterfly feeder right outside your house.

Make someone laugh (or at least crack a smile) every day.

If allowed, bring a couple of balloons to your local children's hospital.

KINDNESS AFFIRMATIONS

I choose to be loving in the face of adversity.

I am emboldened by a soul that's loving and kind.

I hold kindness above all else.

KINDNESS ACTIONS

Whenever you spot a kid's lemonade stand (or any other similar young entrepreneur's venture), make a purchase.

Pick up litter in your neighbourhood park.

For any and all appointments, make it a habit to show up on time, every time.

KINDNESS AFFIRMATIONS

I never give up on the people I love.

I extend my help mindfully and with sensitivity.

I am building a kinder world.

KINDNESS ACTIONS

Know someone who's planning a holiday? Offer to help them get organised and stay on top of everything.

Never stop trying to be a better human being—make a list of 'kindness resolutions.' How can you be a more supportive friend? A more loving partner? A dream teammate?

Leave small plush toys or old tennis balls at a dog park.

KINDNESS AFFIRMATIONS

I honour people's differences and what makes them unique.

There is never anything to be lost in giving.

I refuse to judge others and put people down.

KINDNESS ACTIONS

Offer your seat to someone else on public transport.

Celebrate your friends' milestones! Whether it's a wedding, a showcase for a hobby they're passionate about, a dog adoption day... if it's important to them, be sure to show your unwavering support.

Do a random act of kindness for someone, and challenge them to pay it forward in whatever way they can.

POSITIVE AFFIRMATIONS AND ACTIONS FOR

Health

USE YOUR SELF CARE DAILY RITUALS TO
LEARN TO LOVE YOURSELF, CREATE HAPPINESS,
IMPROVE YOUR CONFIDENCE &
BUILD INNER STRENGTH

Health

Whether you're aware of it or not, your health plays a massive part in your life. In fact, it may very well be at the centre of it all. Working towards your goals, being a blessing to others, enjoying your hobbies and the things you do for fun, and simply being a productive member of society... none of it would be possible if you were unhealthy.

But, what does being healthy really mean? What comes to mind when you think of "health?" Perhaps living an active lifestyle and eating food that's good for you? Or, maybe hitting your ideal weight and getting the body you've always wanted?

In a society that can be hyper-fixated on looks, the physical aspect of health is frequently grossly oversimplified. It is usually whittled down to the bare minimum of an absence of illness and often, maintaining a certain weight and having a 'fit' body.

However, the reality is that looking good is primarily just a sign or 'side effect' of physical health—of your body's systems being in peak condition and all its processes functioning smoothly. While exercise and balanced nutrition are definitely important in achieving and maintaining this, there are so many other factors. These include getting enough good quality sleep and adequate rest, proper hydration, and access to medical support (as needed).

Not only is the idea of physical health limited to such a narrow definition, but even worse, there's also a tendency to disregard all the other aspects of health. While wanting to maintain a particular physique is valid and physical fitness can indeed be an essential component of health, there is so much more to it than just that.

Being healthy also includes mental, emotional, social, and even spiritual wellbeing. All of these are interconnected, and being truly healthy entails understanding and tending to yourself holistically.

First off, mental health is how you process and interpret information and the world around you, including making decisions and managing stress. The term is often used interchangeably with emotional health, but while these certainly overlap, they are not one and the same. As mental health deals with the brain and its functions, you can almost think of it as emotional health's 'physical' counterpart.

On the other hand, emotional health has to do with how you manage feelings. It absolutely doesn't mean always being positive and happy—rather, it's about the ability to deal even with negative emotions. Given that, self-awareness and authenticity play a huge role in emotional health, as these serve as the foundation for developing coping skills to navigate different contexts and situations.

Both mental and emotional dimensions come into play when it comes to our social health or the ability to form meaningful relationships, whether with family, friends, a significant other, or the community at large.

Lastly, the spiritual aspect is possibly one of the most overlooked components of health. Perhaps it's no surprise, as it's not the easiest concept to fit into a singular, neat definition. For many, this could be their practice of faith. For others, it's not necessarily religious, and more a matter of how they fit into the 'big picture'—having that sense of connectedness and purpose.

With this deeper, broader picture of health, it can no doubt be even more daunting to commit to working on your wellbeing. As with anything worthwhile, though, remember that achieving health takes time—it's a process. It's about making one small change at a time, building habits that serve you to replace those that do not.

Along with small-yet-impactful actions, an affirmation practice can be of great help when it comes to health and wellness. Not only does it channel healing energy and strength towards the areas in your life that need it the most, but because your mind, body, heart, and soul are all interconnected, it also empowers you to set positive change in motion across all aspects. Repeating thought patterns that reinforce certain behaviours and beliefs actually makes it easier for you to make healthier choices in your life.

Affirmations also serve as reinforcements for self-care and self-love, two of the most powerful tools in your health and wellbeing journey. The ability to listen to your body and love yourself through it all is so incredibly important.

Each picture of health—and the path to it—is unique. Your goals, milestones, and pace are all wonderfully, gloriously different from everybody else's... and that is beyond okay. No matter where you are on this journey, you deserve to enjoy life and cherish yourself every step of the way.

"Wellness is the complete integration of body, mind, and spirit – the realization that everything we do, think, feel, and believe has an effect on our state of well-being."

- **Greg Anderson**

HEALTH AFFIRMATIONS

I love who I am, and I'm excited about who I am becoming.

I am strong and filled with life.

Energy flows through my body effortlessly.

HEALTH ACTIONS

Begin your day with some energising morning stretches.

Hydrate! Always make sure you are getting enough water throughout the day.

Create a bedtime ritual that helps you wind down and relax. It doesn't have to take long or be complicated—it can be as simple as having a cup of tea or listening to a soothing song.

HEALTH AFFIRMATIONS

My body serves me well.

I honour the shape of my body.

I am happy to be uniquely me.

HEALTH ACTIONS

When you find yourself stressed or anxious, take a moment to pause, close your eyes, and take 10 long, deep breaths.

Try to learn about and get a deeper understanding of what you put on and into your body.

Pick some affirmations that really resonate with you, and practice saying these out loud to yourself in front of the mirror each day.

HEALTH AFFIRMATIONS

I love my body and everything it does for me every day.

I am capable of making healthy decisions for my body and mind.

I deserve to spend time and energy on things that make me happy.

HEALTH ACTIONS

Give yourself at least 10 minutes each day to meditate or practice mindfulness.

Start your day with a hearty, balanced breakfast.

List down 10 things you adore about your body.

HEALTH AFFIRMATIONS

I am at peace with all my body's imperfections.

I am deeply committed to caring for myself.

I am capable of setting healthy boundaries for myself.

HEALTH ACTIONS

Stock your pantry with wholesome, nutritious snacks.

Once a week, treat yourself to something you really, truly enjoy.

Put on some of your favourite upbeat music, turn it up, and dance!

HEALTH AFFIRMATIONS

I am allowed to put myself first.

I am growing and changing in all the ways I am meant to.

I am in control of my wellbeing.

HEALTH ACTIONS

Get your daily dose of vitamin D—sit out in the sunshine for a bit!

Learn a new sport with your partner or a friend.

Do your best to get as much sleep as your body needs. For many, this would be about 7-9 hours nightly.

HEALTH AFFIRMATIONS

I am nourished in both mind and body.

I deserve rest whenever I need it.

I am free to move and be active.

HEALTH ACTIONS

Practice listening to what your body is telling you and responding mindfully to its needs.

It's time to finally get rid of those clothes in the depths of your closet that no longer fit.

Try out a new delicious, nutritious recipe every week.

HEALTH AFFIRMATIONS

I have the power to lift myself up.

I deserve the best health and a fit body.

I honour my inner power.

HEALTH ACTIONS

Run a luxurious bath with your favourite scent and give yourself as much time as you want to enjoy it.

Squeeze in at least 10-15 minutes of exercise every day. It can be as simple as getting your heart rate up with a short walk or doing a few reps of light weights.

As much as possible, avoid screens and blue light an hour before bed.

HEALTH AFFIRMATIONS

I am allowed to be proud of my accomplishments and celebrate these.

I am aging with grace.

I release any stress and tension in both my mind and body.

HEALTH ACTIONS

Make moisturising a post-shower habit—give yourself a little massage while you're at it!

Try out a weekly 'meatless Monday' or 'whole foods Wednesday.'

Bring awareness to your posture, both when sitting and standing.

HEALTH AFFIRMATIONS

Every part of me is worthy of respect.

I let go of thoughts that do not serve me.

I release any expectations I feel pressured to live up to.

HEALTH ACTIONS

Try to enjoy each of your meals mindfully—as much as possible, avoid working lunches and dinners in front of the telly.

Write down the best compliment you've ever received.

Pick up some self-massage techniques online, or even treat yourself to a session with a professional masseuse.

HEALTH AFFIRMATIONS

Every cell in my body is brimming with energy.

I am proud to be a work in progress.

I am a beautiful person inside and out.

HEALTH ACTIONS

Time for a social media audit—unfollow any accounts or influencers that make you feel bad about yourself or don't add any value to your life.

Start that inspirational book that you've been meaning to get around to.

Do an at-home spa day with a DIY face or hair mask.

HEALTH AFFIRMATIONS

My body's systems are all functioning in perfect harmony.

I am in tune with my body and its needs.

Health and wellness flow to me naturally and in abundance.

HEALTH ACTIONS

Remember not to get caught up with measurements or numbers on a scale—focus on feeling happier, healthier, and stronger.

Stretch and strengthen your mind, body, and spirit with some yoga practice.

Let go of any guilt when it comes to food.

HEALTH AFFIRMATIONS

I am filled with grit and determination.

I embrace whatever state of health I am in now.

It's perfectly okay to both work on my body, and at the same time, love it for what it is.

HEALTH ACTIONS

Start a daily mood tracker on your phone or in your journal.

If you have a dog, commit to taking them out for a walk at least once a day. If not, you might even want to consider volunteering to walk a friend's or neighbours.

Whenever possible, choose to take the stairs over the elevator or escalator.

HEALTH AFFIRMATIONS

I deserve all the happiness in the world.

I rise to every challenge in my own unique way.

I am proud to be my own cheerleader.

HEALTH ACTIONS

How long has it been since you've walked barefoot outdoors, on the grass or at the beach?

List down 5 things you're capable of that not many people can do.

Make time to hang out with a friend who's fun to be around.

HEALTH AFFIRMATIONS

Disease, illness, or disability does not define me and what I am capable of.

I am surrounded by people who support my wellbeing.

I am in control of my own happiness.

HEALTH ACTIONS

Have you ever gone a whole day not thinking about what you look like? Challenge yourself to 24 hours without looking at yourself in the mirror, and take note of how it feels.

Commit to keeping a plant or small garden. Set aside time each day to tend to it and enjoy how it flourishes under your care.

Find and learn a breathing exercise that works for you, and use it whenever you need a little pocket of calm in your day.

HEALTH AFFIRMATIONS

My body has the remarkable capacity to heal itself.

Fear cannot stand in my way.

I am patient with my body.

HEALTH ACTIONS

What makes you feel like your best self? List down everything you can think of.

Listen to an uplifting, motivating song. Close your eyes, and enjoy how the music makes you feel.

Hold a board game night with a group of friends or play a couple of brainteaser puzzles with your family.

HEALTH AFFIRMATIONS

I am perfectly imperfect.

I am capable of so much more than I ever dreamed.

I trust in the power of my body.

HEALTH ACTIONS

Pick up a meditative, calming hobby like knitting or mandala-making.

Watch a feel-good movie or a laugh-out-loud sitcom.

Visit your local farmers' market and check out the fresh produce and 'slow' food.

HEALTH AFFIRMATIONS

My body's journey is uniquely mine.

I choose to live in health and vitality.

Healthy habits are a natural part of me.

HEALTH ACTIONS

When was the last time you saw a sunrise? Pick a day to wake up extra early and enjoy the stillness of dawn.

List down 5 healthy boundaries or non-negotiables that you would like to start enforcing.

Plan a camping trip or hike!

HEALTH AFFIRMATIONS

I am allowed to move and grow at my own pace.

I am focused and consistent when it comes to my health.

I am always changing for the better.

HEALTH ACTIONS

If possible, open all your windows and curtains to let fresh air in.

Try a freewriting exercise. No (over) thinking—just put your pen to paper and write from your stream of consciousness.

The next time a negative thought about yourself pops into your head, imagine saying it to or about someone you love. Chances are, you'll be able to turn that thought right around.

HEALTH AFFIRMATIONS

I listen to my body and tend to its needs.

I only get stronger and fitter every day.

I choose to live harmoniously and in perfect balance.

HEALTH ACTIONS

Re-evaluate your relationships. Ask yourself if it might be time to let go of or stop investing emotionally in those that bring toxicity and negativity into your life.

Put up some blackout curtains to improve the quality of your sleep.

Look up ways to incorporate essential oils into your day. There are options for a variety of uses, from stress-busting and relaxation to boosting energy.

HEALTH AFFIRMATIONS

I am thriving and vibrantly alive.

I send my energy towards my wellbeing.

Every healthy choice I make counts.

HEALTH ACTIONS

Build a daily journaling habit, taking stock of all aspects of your wellbeing, from physical to emotional.

Give yourself permission to say 'no' to something.

Battle the afternoon slump with a 20-minute power nap.

HEALTH AFFIRMATIONS

My body loves and supports me.

I am in a constant state of healing.

I have everything it takes to achieve my fittest self.

HEALTH ACTIONS

Encourage friends and family to join you in your fitness journey!

Look into healthy food swaps you can easily, sustainably incorporate into your diet.

Write down 3 things you don't like about yourself. Then, rewrite them into positive, affirming statements.

HEALTH AFFIRMATIONS

My mind and body are powerfully, wholly connected.

I am worthy of wellbeing.

I allow my breath to fuel and move me.

HEALTH ACTIONS

Stay on top of your annual physical check-ups—when it comes to health, preventive measures go a long way!

List down 5 things that boost your energy and 5 things that drain it. Take what you learn from this quick exercise into the rest of your week.

Stay on track and motivated by joining a fitness community, even just online.

HEALTH AFFIRMATIONS

I am willing to make healthy changes for myself.

I free myself from any habits that harm me.

I am fully committed to a healthy, balanced life.

HEALTH ACTIONS

Replace 2-3 snacks or desserts a week with fruit and veg.

Once a week, make cooking dinner a family activity!

Create a go-to workout playlist with all your favourite upbeat songs.

HEALTH AFFIRMATIONS

I deserve rest and recovery.

I grant my body the grace it needs to grow and flourish in health.

I love how it feels to be active.

HEALTH ACTIONS

Do you have a bad habit you've been meaning to kick? It's time to buckle down and get serious about it—you can do this!

Set realistic goals and set up sustainable healthy habits. Remember, the journey matters as much (if not more than) the destination.

Sign up for a fun run or another physical event you've always wanted to try and commit to training for it.

HEALTH AFFIRMATIONS

I am not afraid to continue to explore and expand what my body can do.

I am transforming into the healthiest version of myself.

I cultivate a healthy mind and inner self.

HEALTH ACTIONS

Before bed, listen to some ambient sleep sounds like recordings of rain or waves crashing on the beach.

Incorporate natural elements such as wood, fresh flowers, or even a small water feature into your indoor space.

Shake up your fitness routine with a new workout once a week.

POSITIVE AFFIRMATIONS AND ACTIONS FOR BUILDING YOUR
Side Hustle
PRACTICE POSITIVITY AND BUILD AN
ENTREPRENEUR'S MINDSET WITH
DAILY RITUALS AND MANIFESTING

Side Hustle

When it comes to a career or business, success can look like so many different things to different people. For some, it could mean working your way up the corporate ladder and clinching that top spot. For others, it could mean being able to turn your passion into a lucrative venture. It could even be as broad as achieving financial independence.

No matter what your picture of success is, there's no denying that getting there doesn't happen overnight—it's a journey filled with challenges, setbacks, and, yes, sometimes, even failures.

Navigating that journey demands certain qualities of us. Contemplate the people you consider to have absolutely, unquestionably achieved success. What are they like? How do they think? What do they believe, and how does that manifest in their work?

Regardless of field or industry, you'll find that the most successful people have one thing in common: an entrepreneurial mindset.

In a nutshell, the entrepreneurial mindset is the ability to identify opportunities and take steps to maximise these. This may sound like a tall order, but this is actually underpinned by certain core values and qualities that extend even beyond business and succeeding in your professional life.

First, passion and motivation are key to succeeding as an entrepreneur. Again, the road to your goals won't always be smooth. To get through those tough times, you need that inner fire and drive—persistence and hard work are only possible when these come from a place deep within you.

Creativity is also an important ingredient of the entrepreneurial mindset. Now, this doesn't necessarily mean 'artistic.' Essentially, it's the ability to take existing ideas and insights to come up with something new. Creative thinking comes into play across so many different things, from finding solutions to business challenges, finding more efficient ways to do things, and forging new paths.

Successful people also exhibit a willingness to learn. Any idea—even the best of the best—can always be better, and a great entrepreneur is always open to constructive input from other people. Also, this openness is what will enable you to use mistakes to your advantage; through the lens of learning.

Lastly, and perhaps most importantly, is self-belief. A huge part of being a successful entrepreneur is getting people on board with you—how would you manage to do that if you aren't a hundred per cent on board yourself? How is anybody else supposed to believe in you if you don't? Being confident in the value you offer will inspire the same confidence in others, whether its customers or business partners. Self-belief comes from a strong sense of who you are, where you stand, and what you stand for. Any venture requires a degree of risk at some point—having this foundation makes you unshakeable, or at the very least, resilient.

With everything else on your plate, though, it can be hard to see yourself taking the time out to work on all of these qualities and hone your skills further. But, think of it this way: deliberately working on developing an entrepreneur's mindset is an active investment in yourself and your business.

And, it can be as simple as spending a few minutes on an affirmation practice each day. Being a business owner can pull you in several different directions at any given moment. There is always something to do, a conversation to be had, a decision that has to be made. Affirmations can help you re-centre and go back to what truly matters. These can be powerful tools to stay focused—on your goals, the foundation you are rooting from, and the tools you are sharpening to aid you on your journey.

Especially for self-belief, affirmations can be an amazing way to unlock and cultivate the entrepreneurial mindset. There's a reason it's called an affirmation practice—the very mechanism behind affirmations can be compared to working out or physical training. By repeating positive thought patterns, you reinforce certain connections and functions in your brain. Through time, these become easier to access and tap into.

Success—whatever that may be to you—starts within. You already have everything you need. All that's left to do is plant the seeds with thought, water them with action, and before you know it, you'll be reaping the fruits of your efforts.

"Every time you state what you want or believe, you're the first to hear it. It's a message to both you and others about what you think is possible. Don't put a ceiling on yourself."

- Oprah Winfrey

ENTREPRENEUR MINDSET AFFIRMATIONS

I see every day as an opportunity.

I am capable of great things.

I am on an amazing journey towards my goals.

ENTREPRENEUR MINDSET ACTIONS

Write down your biggest, boldest dreams. Don't be afraid to get as specific and detailed as you want!

Commit to learning something new, whether it's a skill, a hobby, or even just an interesting new concept or fact.

Think of someone you look up to—perhaps a leader in your field, or someone whose success you aspire for—and try to list down the qualities you admire in them.

ENTREPRENEUR MINDSET AFFIRMATIONS

Every day takes me closer to my goals.

I am skilled, intelligent, and competent.

I surround myself with people who share my drive and values.

ENTREPRENEUR MINDSET ACTIONS

Create a vision board and display it somewhere you can always see.

Do at least one thing every day that counts towards your goals.

Take a long walk while listening to a podcast that interests or inspires you.

ENTREPRENEUR MINDSET AFFIRMATIONS

I am worthy of the success I envision for myself.

I believe in my abilities and power to succeed.

I am filled with boundless potential.

ENTREPRENEUR MINDSET ACTIONS

Clear the clutter from your physical or digital workspace.

Write down what success means to you. What does it look like? What does it feel like?

List down 5 skills or abilities you are proud to have.

ENTREPRENEUR MINDSET AFFIRMATIONS

There are no limits to what I am capable of.

I have what it takes to overcome any challenge that comes my way.

I am great at channelling positive energy into action.

ENTREPRENEUR MINDSET ACTIONS

Celebrate even little wins—it can be as simple as treating yourself to a scoop of ice cream for getting through a long workday.

Think about the toughest challenge you've taken on at work. How did you overcome it, and how did you feel afterwards?

When faced with a tough situation that requires a decision or response, always take a moment to absorb and reflect before moving into action.

ENTREPRENEUR MINDSET AFFIRMATIONS

I trust my own judgment.

I have the ability to make good decisions.

I am focused and motivated.

ENTREPRENEUR MINDSET ACTIONS

Challenge yourself to try something you've always wanted to do but have been too afraid to.

Put together a daily or weekly checklist of small-yet-impactful, realistic, and achievable wins. Don't forget to tick items off as you go along!

Dress for success, whatever it means to you. It doesn't necessarily have to mean 'fancy'—as long as it makes you feel confident and in control, you're all set.

ENTREPRENEUR MINDSET AFFIRMATIONS

I am supported by people who care about me and want me to achieve my goals.

I am inspired and empowered in my journey towards success.

Abundance flows naturally to me.

ENTREPRENEUR MINDSET ACTIONS

Even during the busiest of days, don't forget to take breaks. Even just for 10 minutes a time, allow yourself to step away from work and rest or do something completely unrelated.

Put on some upbeat, energising music to kick-start your workday!

Be someone's accountability partner and have them be yours. Check-in with each other regularly to share updates on your progress towards your respective goals.

ENTREPRENEUR MINDSET AFFIRMATIONS

I have all the tools that I need to make my dreams a reality.

Everything that I need to succeed is already within me.

I am passionate about my dreams.

ENTREPRENEUR MINDSET ACTIONS

Take a negative thought, comment, or situation and challenge yourself to turn it into something positive.

Make it a daily habit to read a few pages—or better yet, a whole chapter—of any book of your choice.

Choose one of your biggest goals and create a 90-day action plan for it. This doesn't necessarily mean you have to reach the goal itself in 90 days—you simply have to take significant strides towards it.

ENTREPRENEUR MINDSET AFFIRMATIONS

I am in a prime position to prosper.

Money flows to me in abundance.

I am deserving of the wealth I desire.

ENTREPRENEUR MINDSET ACTIONS

Close your eyes and imagine the future you want for yourself. Really try to picture where you'll be, what you'll be doing, and even the things you'll have.

Join social groups that share your passions and give yourself opportunities to engage with equally ambitious and motivated people.

Reach out to and connect with people you can learn from—you can even look into tapping mentors or coaches for your specific goals.

ENTREPRENEUR MINDSET AFFIRMATIONS

I am always eager to learn and discover new things.

I am not afraid to ask questions.

I am open to diverse ideas.

ENTREPRENEUR MINDSET ACTIONS

Make it a habit to jot down your random thoughts, ideas, and questions—you never know what future potential these may hold.

Visit a local exhibition or museum and just soak everything in.

When spending long hours working seated, make sure to get up and move around every once in a while. Take a couple of minutes to stretch out your arms, legs, neck and back.

ENTREPRENEUR MINDSET AFFIRMATIONS

I am someone the best of the best would like to work with.

I am in charge of my life and my success.

I do not let stumbling blocks discourage me.

ENTREPRENEUR MINDSET ACTIONS

Strike up a conversation with someone you wouldn't usually have the chance to talk to—there's something to learn from everyone.

Shake things up with a change in scenery—try taking your work outdoors or, at the very least, to a different spot in your house.

Write about your proudest moment or most significant achievement.

ENTREPRENEUR MINDSET AFFIRMATIONS

I am exactly the kind of leader that I want to be.

I am an overflowing spring of great ideas.

I am a bold, creative, innovative thinker.

ENTREPRENEUR MINDSET ACTIONS

What's something you can do today that will make you feel like the person you aspire to be 5 years from now? Do it.

Spend an afternoon immersed in a creative activity you enjoy without worrying about the output.

Update your resume and get your professional profile or portfolio in order.

ENTREPRENEUR MINDSET AFFIRMATIONS

I welcome growth and positive change.

I release self-doubt.

I open myself up to opportunities and abundance.

ENTREPRENEUR MINDSET ACTIONS

Include setting an intention for the day in your morning ritual.

Wrap up your workday by jotting down a quick to-do list that will help you hit the ground running on the following day.

Try to never hit the snooze button.

ENTREPRENEUR MINDSET AFFIRMATIONS

I am confident in my abilities.

I am steadfast in my determination to reach my goals.

I define and shape my own picture of success.

ENTREPRENEUR MINDSET ACTIONS

Write about a moment when you felt on top of the world—confident, in control, and amazing.

Learn a new language! No need to worry about mastering it or even becoming conversational—just go at your own pace and enjoy the process.

Define your support system. List down people you can count on, with the specific things you know they can help you with.

ENTREPRENEUR MINDSET AFFIRMATIONS

I am adaptable and resilient.

I can handle whatever challenges come my way.

I don't need everything to go my way to succeed.

ENTREPRENEUR MINDSET ACTIONS

Read an inspirational biography or autobiography.

Write about the word 'confidence.' What does it mean to you? How does it feel? What are some ways you can cultivate it in yourself?

Get your budget and finances in order and commit to tracking these religiously.

ENTREPRENEUR MINDSET AFFIRMATIONS

I've got all the smarts and savvy I need.

I put my heart into everything I do.

My best is enough.

ENTREPRENEUR MINDSET ACTIONS

Declutter your inbox.

What's your favourite inspirational or motivational quote? Write it down and consider using it as your desktop or phone wallpaper.

When discussing ideas at work or brainstorming with your team, practice saying "Yes, and…" instead of "No."

ENTREPRENEUR MINDSET AFFIRMATIONS

I know when and how to ask for help when I need it.

I actively learn from others who know more than I do.

I will succeed without compromising my values and beliefs.

ENTREPRENEUR MINDSET ACTIONS

Challenge yourself to overcome mental barriers. What would you be doing if failure weren't a possibility?

List down 10 things you want to learn.

Find ways to share your passions with others. Is there anyone interested in learning from or being mentored by you? Reach out to them.

ENTREPRENEUR MINDSET AFFIRMATIONS

I am willing to put in the work to make my dreams come true.

I am unstoppable in pursuit of my goals.

I am not afraid to try.

ENTREPRENEUR MINDSET ACTIONS

List down 5 things you've done this week that have brought you closer to your goals.

What's one difficult conversation you've been putting off? Can you work towards finally having it soon?

Be vocal about your goals—tell someone close to you all about what you're aiming to achieve and how you're planning to get there.

ENTREPRENEUR MINDSET AFFIRMATIONS

As long as I do my best, everything will turn out as it should.

I release any worry or anxiety about the future.

I am the author of my life story.

ENTREPRENEUR MINDSET ACTIONS

Write down one thing you are struggling with, and 5 things you are doing (or plan to do) to overcome it.

If possible, find ways to arrange your schedule in a manner that honours whether you're a morning or night person.

Get out of your comfort zone and attend an industry event where you can expand your professional network.

ENTREPRENEUR MINDSET AFFIRMATIONS

I am not defined by past mistakes.

I am capable of turning roadblocks into stepping-stones.

There is nothing standing in the way of my success.

ENTREPRENEUR MINDSET ACTIONS

Describe what you think the experience is or would be like for someone who works for you.

Do some research on quick tips and lifehacks that are relevant to your field or business.

Volunteer for a career day talk at a local school.

ENTREPRENEUR MINDSET AFFIRMATIONS

I will not allow my spark to be dimmed.

My vision of the future is clear and vivid.

I am right where I need to be at this point in my life.

ENTREPRENEUR MINDSET ACTIONS

Write about how you are making the world a better place in your own way.

Think back to your childhood. What did you want to be when you grew up? Write about why that was your dream.

Ask someone you consider successful for one piece of career or life advice.

ENTREPRENEUR MINDSET AFFIRMATIONS

I will show up for myself and for my dreams.

I am clearing the path towards wealth and success.

I bring my own unique perspective to the table.

ENTREPRENEUR MINDSET ACTIONS

Set up a system of tracking your goals. It could be a journal, an app, or even just a spreadsheet—don't worry if it takes some trial and error to find what works for you.

Even when they're different from the consensus, practice speaking up and voicing your opinions politely but firmly.

Draw out a word cloud or mind map with 'success' as the centre.

ENTREPRENEUR MINDSET AFFIRMATIONS

I am a valued asset to those I work with.

I do not shy away from my own greatness.

I stand in the light unafraid.

ENTREPRENEUR MINDSET ACTIONS

What do you usually spend most of your time on? How about the least time? As an experiment, track your time for a day and see what you can learn from the exercise.

What do you consider your core values? Write them down, and from your list, try to create a personal mantra.

Look into any certifications relevant to your field and consider working towards one.

ENTREPRENEUR MINDSET AFFIRMATIONS

Every day, I only get better
and better at what I do.

I continuously hone my craft
and sharpen my skills.

I am brimming with joyful
anticipation for what I am yet
to achieve.

ENTREPRENEUR MINDSET ACTIONS

List down 5 of your worst work and productivity habits. What steps can you take to break them?

Define your 'why.' List down the people and things that motivate you and keep you going in your journey towards success.

Train yourself to respond with "I'll try" every time you're tempted to think or say "I can't".

ENTREPRENEUR MINDSET AFFIRMATIONS

My ideas can make a difference in the world.

I stay the course, even when things don't go as planned.

I am built for success.

ENTREPRENEUR MINDSET ACTIONS

Let go of past mistakes by listing down 5 of what you consider your 'failures' or regrets. Then, physically crumple up that piece of paper and throw it away.

If you work on a computer, try using a standing desk for a few hours each day.

List down 5 ways you make your boss', team or client's life easier.

ENTREPRENEUR MINDSET AFFIRMATIONS

I move through life with purpose.

I embrace and enjoy every phase of my journey.

My life's best is still to come.

ENTREPRENEUR MINDSET ACTIONS

Find a digital organisation, labelling, and filing system that works for you.

As much as possible, avoid working overtime or allowing work to make its way into personal or family time.

Although it can be challenging, respond to constructive feedback with an open mind—always starting with "I hear you, thank you," is a great habit to practice.

Also available by **Kathy Shanks**...

Guided Journaling is available worldwide as print or ebook at Amazon, Booktopia, Barnes & Noble and all good bookstores.

Also available in Australia from **turtlepublishing.com.au**

Inside this book you'll discover how to use my method of journaling to:

- Work towards creating balance for heart, mind, body and soul without sacrificing career and relationships
- Create rituals that help you develop gratitude
- Use daily affirmations to practice positivity and manifest your future dreams
- Discover strategies to improve your relationships, build your life mission, start a side hustle, discover yourself, develop self-love, improve your health AND improve your mindset

It seems too good to be true, right! Organising your thoughts and dreams in 10-20 minutes a day can be that one simple change that actually makes your dreams become a reality.

Make your journal your safe haven, a place of nurturing for you to come and reflect, clear your mind, set goals, develop gratitude, make plans, dream, and take steps towards the future that has always seemed just out of reach.

> Please join our journaling community at
> **facebook.com/groups/kathyshanks**
> for exclusive insider access to updates and releases

Also available in the
Guided Journaling Series...

Journaling for a
Balanced Life with a
Health focus

Journaling for a
Balanced Life with a
Life Mission focus

Journaling for a
Balanced Life with a
focus on the **Heart**

Journaling for a
Balanced Life with a
Gratitude & Manifest focus

We have a selection of *journals* available worldwide as
print or ebook at Amazon, Booktopia,
Barnes & Noble and all good bookstores.
Also available in Australia from **turtlepublishing.com.au**

www.ingramcontent.com/pod-product-compliance
Lightning Source LLC
Chambersburg PA
CBHW020317010526
44107CB00054B/1871